Historic Catholic Churches of Northeastern New Mexico

HISTORIC CATHOLIC CHURCHES OF NORTHEASTERN NEW MEXICO

DAVID POLICANSKY

SUNSTONE
PRESS

SANTA FE

On the front cover: San Francisco de Asís Catholic Church, Ranchos de Taos
On the back cover: Catholic Chapel of San Isidro, Tinaja

Sunstone books may be purchased for educational, business, or sales promotional use.
For information please write: Special Markets Department, Sunstone Press,
P.O. Box 2321, Santa Fe, New Mexico 87504-2321.
Printed on acid-free paper
∞

LIBRARY OF CONGRESS CATALOGING IN PUBLICATION DATA

(ON FILE)

DEDICATION

I dedicate this book to all the individuals and communities that care for and cherish their historic churches.
Long may they and their churches endure.

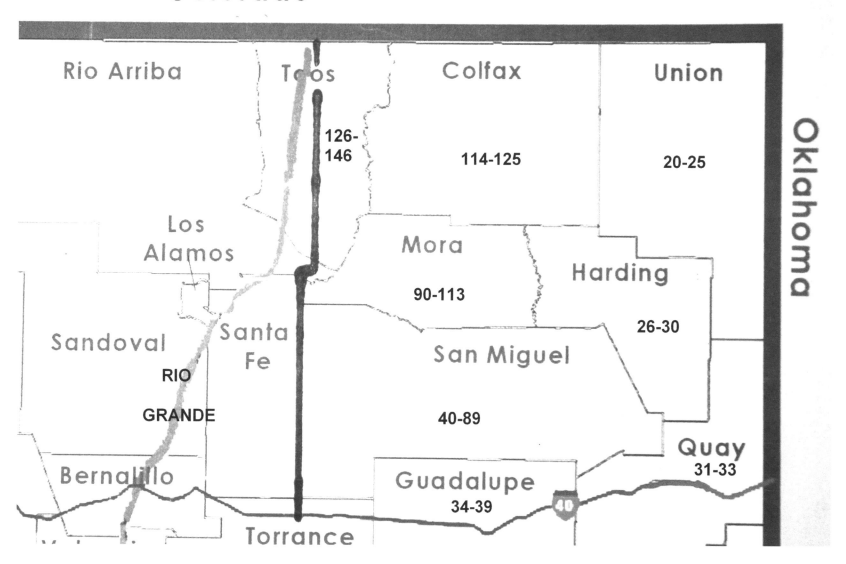

Map of approximate locations of churches in this book. The numbers in each county are the pages where each church is illustrated and briefly described, and location information is given. The arrangement of churches in the book is intended to facilitate planning road trips to see groups of them.

CONTENTS

INTRODUCTION

Catholic churches, more than other denominations of organized religion, are an enormous part of New Mexico's history, culture, and landscapes. When European settlement of New Mexico began in 1598—earlier than in any other U.S. state except Florida—the Spanish Franciscans introduced the indigenous inhabitants to Catholicism, and New Mexico was changed forever. These Hispanic people were Catholics themselves, and until 1853, when a Baptist church was established in Santa Fe, Catholicism remained the only organized Christian religion in the state. The history of the interactions between Catholicism and the religions of New Mexico's indigenous inhabitants, as well as with the Spanish and Mexican and later U.S. rulers of New Mexico, has been long, complicated, and sometimes ugly. But it is quintessentially New Mexican. It explains why other Christian denominations weren't established here until after New Mexico became a U.S. territory in 1848, and it influenced the types of Catholic churches that are in New Mexico and where they are today. The role of Catholicism in New Mexico's history is dealt with more extensively in several of the books in the Selected Further Readings toward the end of this book.

Old Catholic churches are all over New Mexico, and each of them has a story. Like the churches, each story is unique. Most of them involve communities, families, individual memories, and a sense of place. The stories include weddings, births, baptisms, confirmations, communions, deaths and funerals, parents and grandparents, aunts and uncles, hard times and good times, feast days, deterioration of the building, repair, restoration, and rebuilding; all the things that give the churches character and make

them so important to their communities. It is these stories that explain, at least in part, why so many small, rural churches in New Mexico continue to survive against all odds.

There are more than four hundred historic Catholic churches in New Mexico, and I have tried to find and photograph all of them. That might be a never-ending mission, but I think that I have photographed at least a large majority of them. I wish I could tell the story of each of them, too. However, that is not this book, which presents photographs and brief descriptions of each church and directions to find them. Nonetheless, I hope readers will remember that each of these churches has a story, and how important the stories are.

My first book, *Historic Catholic Churches Along the Rio Grande in New Mexico*, focuses on the churches along and near the Rio Grande; the second, *Historic Catholic Churches of Central and Southern New Mexico*, covers Catholic churches in the rest of central and southern New Mexico. This book covers northeastern New Mexico, as described below, again with a cut-off date for church construction of 1955. Also included are a few others of relevance or design or historic value, even though they are more recent. This book follows the general format of the first two, but each book is different from the others. Each time I do one of these books, I learn more: more about Catholic churches, more about New Mexico, more about the communities and individuals that care for their churches, more about photography, and more about the churches' importance in New Mexico's natural, social, and cultural landscapes. This learning is reflected in the books' contents. Also, each book covers a distinct set of landscapes, cultures, and architecture. Northern New Mexico has more old Catholic churches than the rest of the state, and to keep the books' sizes manageable I divided it into two parts: the northeast (this book) and the northwest.

Once again, I have used Interstate Highway 40 as the divider between central and southern New Mexico and northern New Mexico. Because that highway isn't straight, some unavoidable arbitrariness results in the division. The east-west divide I chose was the Santa Fe-San Miguel county line from Interstate 40 to Mora County, and from there to the Colorado border, the divider is slightly to the east: the line of 105⁰ 39' West (105.65⁰ West), marked in DeLorme's *New Mexico Atlas and Gazetteer* (reading list). The result is the churches around Santa Fe and much of the High Road to Taos are in the northwest, while the churches in and around Taos are in this book.

As in my previous books, the churches are arranged by county. The counties are not arranged in alphabetical order (except, of course, in the index), but instead begin with Union County in the far northeast, then continue south to Harding and Quay counties, then Guadalupe, San Miguel, Mora, and Colfax counties as the next tier of counties to the west, and finally Taos County. I hope this arrangement, although it is somewhat arbitrary, facilitates road trips to see some of the churches in this book by putting adjacent churches close to each other. I have provided directions to most of the churches in the captions for the images of them that should be detailed enough to make finding them fairly easy. However, I have not provided detailed directions for all churches that are behind locked gates. San Miguel County is the winner with 47 churches, followed by Mora County with 23; the part of Taos County in this book has 20. Adding the rest brings the total in this book to 117 churches.

Some churches are easy to find; San Francisco de Asís in Ranchos de Taos (pages 142 and 143) is a notable example. Just off paved New Mexico Highway 68, it is spectacular, and according to Wikipedia, it is the most-photographed church in the United States. Others, such as the Chapel of San Isidro in Tinaja, Colfax County (page 118), require traveling many miles on remote, unpaved roads and are not easy to find. A few are behind locked gates, and before I could find them, I had to find the people who had the keys. While finding such remote churches gives me a great feeling of achievement, and satisfaction in knowing that through these photographs people who never would see them otherwise can appreciate these treasures, I expect that most readers will content themselves with visiting churches that are easier to reach.

Many of the people I've met as I've traveled New Mexico searching out historic Catholic churches have been kind, interesting, and eager to show me their churches, many of which have been cared for by members of their family for generations. It is hard to overemphasize the degree to which many rural churches depend for their survival on dedicated individuals and communities, and it is hard not to wonder what will happen to them as rural depopulation continues in New Mexico and church membership continues to decline. The kindness of these people and others, and the pride they have in their churches have been an inspiration to me, and a motivation to document these churches as well as I can. This and my previous books are products of this motivation.

The more time I spend finding and photographing old Catholic churches and meeting the people who love and care for them, the clearer it becomes that New Mexico's current blend of Native American, Hispanic, Anglo, and Catholic traditions is uniquely fascinating, and that the buildings in these photographs reflect that blend. Furthermore, as I see many rural churches that once served dozens of people but now serve maybe only a handful or fewer, it also is clear that these buildings, which reflect so much cultural history, are disappearing. Most of the larger, iconic churches will likely survive, but many of the smaller and more-remote ones might not. Indeed, many of them already have disappeared, and too many are in disrepair. I hope that drawing attention to them as my books do can broaden the constituency of people who value them and can contribute to their continued survival. At a minimum, I hope that these books will inspire readers to explore, cherish, and enjoy New Mexico's glorious landscapes.

—Mountainair, New Mexico, 2023.

Finding and Photographing New Mexico's Old Churches

New Mexico has great richness and diversity in its Catholic churches, although none has the opulence of those in Europe and in Latin America. Many of New Mexico's older Catholic churches are along and near waterways. In addition to the Rio Grande, the Chama, Mimbres, Mora, Pecos, and other rivers and their tributaries have many wonderful churches along and near them. Even some churches that are reached by dirt roads through rugged terrain turn out to be near streams. Most New Mexico streams do not have roads along much of their distance, and so other than the Rio Grande and parts of the Chama, Mimbres, Mora, and Pecos rivers, planning to drive along them is not an effective way to find churches. But there are other methods, including using this and my previous books, which provide detailed directions to almost all of the churches in them. Some other books cited here also are quite helpful in finding churches, as are websites, pamphlets, friends, and acquaintances. If you know someone who has lived in an area for a while, ask about nearby churches. Then there is old-fashioned exploration. Do you see a place name on a map at the end of a road, or a road that passes through interesting areas? Go there. Be careful that you and your vehicle can handle the roads and the conditions, but much of the time you will be rewarded, if not by a gem of a church, then by wonderful scenery. And there still will be detective work after you find a church; sometimes its name and often its construction date are not easy to find.

Two rules are important. The first is that you should please be respectful of private property and of local communities and their inhabitants, including pueblos. In my experience, people in small communities are proud of their churches and will gladly show them to you and tell you what they know about them. Be careful before photographing churches. Most of the time, photographs of the outside of a church are fine, but if someone unlocks a church for you, ask before photographing the interior. Be particularly careful in pueblos. Some allow photography of buildings; some require permits for any photography, and others prohibit photography within the pueblo entirely. Please obey all posted signs in pueblos. When you visit them, you are their guest.

The second rule concerns navigation. All U.S. and state highways in New Mexico, as in most U.S. states, have mile-markers that start at zero at their southern or western origin or entry into the state; the numbers increase toward the north and east. For example, Interstate 25 begins at mile-marker zero at its origin at Interstate 10 near Las Cruces, and the numbers increase as you go north; Interstate 40 begins at mile-marker zero where it enters New Mexico at the Arizona border and the numbers increase as you head east. Exit numbers on highways match the mile-markers as closely as possible. But the numbering of highways can change from time to time, so make sure you have current highway information.

Many of the county roads and even a few state highways mentioned in my books are unpaved. Some are good gravel roads, but others are rough and cross arroyos, and they can be difficult in wet, muddy, snowy, or sometimes even in dry conditions. Those roads require high-clearance or four-wheel-drive vehicles. In addition, many of the roads traverse open range, which means you can encounter cattle at any time. Slow is better than fast on such roads. Furthermore, some of these roads pass through private property. In most cases access is permitted as long as you stay on the road. I take closed but unlocked gates on county roads as permission to continue, but it is essential to close any gate you open as soon as you have passed through it. Gates usually are closed to prevent unwanted movements of animals. Whether a landowner is legally permitted to block access on a county road is beyond my expertise, but I advise against forcing the issue. If I encounter a locked gate blocking access to a church, I try to find a person who will unlock it for me, a sometimes challenging and time-consuming but so far always rewarding endeavor. The directions in this book are current as of the publication date, but things can change.

Photographing churches is a delightful challenge. For my books, I have tried to represent each church by a single photograph of the exterior, with an interior photograph in some cases. This has meant omitting various interesting or pleasing aspects of many churches, but my aim here has been to present the best aspect of each church while also providing an illustration that helps you to identify the church. For this reason, I have tried to include the front of the church in each photograph.

Usually, a church looks best when the light is on the front. Some churches face south, and they are a photographer's dream, because they have good light most of the day. But more churches face east than other directions, and some even face north, which means they seldom have good light, and then only in summer. I have been lucky to find some remote churches that required difficult travel over rough roads bathed in glorious light on my first visit, but sometimes I have visited a church twice or even three times to get good light. In a few cases, I just accepted light that wasn't the best.

Another challenge can be presented by a church's surroundings, which might prevent one from getting to the best place for a photograph. These obstacles include fences, gates, telephone poles, other buildings, ditches, vehicles, private property, unfavorable topography, and other things. You do the best you can.

Many small, rural churches are in need of funds for maintenance and restoration, so please consider donating to them if given an opportunity. And be prepared to meet many dogs, which seem to abound around old, rural churches.

For those interested in technical details, my main camera is a 20.2-megapixel Canon EOS 6D with a Canon EF 24-105 mm f/3.5-5.6 IS STM lens. This provides wide-angle to medium-telephoto views. The camera also handles high ISOs well, so I never use flash inside any church. For harder-to-reach, more-distant churches, I use a Canon 100-400 mm f/4.5-5.6L IS II lens.

ABOUT CHURCH NAMES
AND CONSTRUCTION DATES

San Antonio de Padua Catholic Church in Valdez (page 133) is given a construction date in one source as middle 1900s, in another as 1840, and the sign in front of the church says 1823. Agua Negra Presbyterian Church in Holman (page 106) is described as San Isidro Catholic Church built in the 1950s in one of those sources, and as San Isidro but built in the early 1900s in another. There are other examples of such discrepancies as well. Which, if any, of those names and dates are correct?

Correctly identifying the name of a church and its construction date has obviously challenged more people than only me. Let's start with names. Sometimes a church's name is written on or next to it, but sometimes it is nowhere to be seen. The challenge is increased when a church changes its name, which is not that rare, or when it has two names, or when it is referred to in English versus in Spanish. Some church names are quite common in New Mexico, so for example there are many churches named for San Antonio, San Isidro, San José, Nuestra Señora de Guadalupe, and others. In addition to church names, many place names also are repeated in New Mexico and hence names like Los Alamos or San Miguel refer to more than one locality. In general, I have used the name as it appears on a church—if it appears—and I have used place names as they appear on highway signs or in DeLorme's *New Mexico Atlas and Gazetteer* or Julyan's *The Place Names of New Mexico* (reading list). I also have consulted historical documents, parishes, Internet sources, and local residents for church and place names.

Construction dates also are challenging to specify accurately. Sometimes a church will have a sign saying "Established on such and such a date," but that date might refer to the establishment of the parish or mission that the church belongs to and not of the building itself. Sometimes there is only a date, and that too might—or might not—refer to the date the building was constructed. Sometimes the date at the church conflicts with other information. It is for such reasons (as well as simple mistakes) that different sources give different names and construction dates for some churches. In addition, major renovations or even rebuilds often aren't noted on church signs. In this book, two dates separated by a slash (e.g., 1857/1929) indicate an initial build date and a date of major restoration or rebuilding.

What about San Antonio in Valdez and San Isidro/Agua Negra in Holman? For the former, the context—the presence of other churches nearby built in the early 1800s—and the church's appearance make it likely that early 1800s is correct, and not middle 1900s. So I accepted the date (1823) on the sign in front of the church. The identification problems of Agua Negra in Holman are discussed briefly on pages 106 and 107. Long-time residents of the area around Holman as well as historical documents indicate that there was a Presbytarian church in the area, formerly known as Agua Negra, as early as 1905. Thus, in this book, it's Agua Negra Presbyterian Church, late 1800s or early 1900s.

It is a wonder that more errors aren't made. I have done my best to eliminate errors, by cross-checking sources; by asking questions of locals, parishes, diocesan historians, and others (please see the acknowledgments); and by reading as many documents as I can find. I have tried to be transparent about uncertainties. But despite my best efforts, it is likely that I too have made errors. For those, I ask the reader's indulgence.

SUGGESTED ROAD TRIPS TO SEE OLD CHURCHES

Finding old Catholic churches in New Mexico is a rewarding activity, because doing so takes you to some lovely places that you might not visit otherwise. In my book on central and southern New Mexico churches I suggested specific road trips to see churches, but the density of historic Catholic churches in this region—especially in Mora, San Miguel, and Taos counties—is too great to suggest specific road trips. However, some highways or combinations of highways have many churches along them. Interstate 25, and New Mexico highways 3, 94, 105, 120, 442, 518, and 522 are particularly rewarding routes. Nearby Rio Arriba, Santa Fe, and more-western parts of Taos counties, covered or to be covered in others of my books, also have many historic Catholic churches. Las Vegas, Mora, and Taos are great bases for expeditions to see historic churches in northeastern New Mexico.

THE CHALLENGE OF PRESERVING AND RESTORING OLD CHURCHES

It should be clear from this and other books and from driving around the countryside that the survival of many historic Catholic churches in New Mexico is far from assured. Indeed, dozens if not hundreds have disappeared over the past four centuries, for a variety of reasons. Frank Graziano (see reading list) addressed this issue in detail. In its simplest terms, the problem results from lack of funds for maintenance and repair, and that results from the depopulation of rural communities, the decline in adherence to Catholicism, conversion to other denominations, and improved transportation. The role of the last factor might not be obvious. Before the 1930s, travel in rural areas was difficult, and so people in small communities built churches where they lived rather than travel to a distant one. Now transportation is much easier, and there aren't enough priests to serve all the churches, so parishioners can get to the parish church more easily than previously. An objective observer might conclude that there are too many Catholic churches in New Mexico today.

Graziano discussed an additional challenge for obtaining adequate funding, namely the tension between parish and diocesan administrations, which own the mission churches, but which don't have the funds, or the willingness to provide the funds, to maintain them; and the remaining congregations of the mission churches, whose members regard them as "their" churches. The parishes also require the missions' congregations to pay for insurance, making funds that might be used for maintenance and repair unavailable. The topic is critical for understanding the genesis of the funding problem, and I refer the reader to Graziano's book. He did discuss possible solutions, and those considerations led him to found Nuevo Mexico Profundo (see below).

It seems likely that not all small, rural, Catholic churches in New Mexico will endure. There just are not sufficient resources for all of the churches that need them. And restoring a church once is not enough: it needs to be maintained. If it is not, it will need restoration again, or it will fall into ruin. But there is hope for many of them, and that hope lies in part in the organizations mentioned below.

Many individuals and organizations are interested in preserving New Mexico's history, culture, and architecture, including its old Catholic churches, but, as described above, not much money is available in many cases. Preserving old churches often depends on community and family efforts. Many churches have a *mayordomo* or *mayordoma*, an individual who takes responsibility for taking care of and maintaining the church. Historically, these people were elected from the congregation or community each year, but today many of them maintain the role for years, or even decades, because nobody is available to take their place. They sometimes can help organizing fundraising and restoration efforts. Many small churches have collection boxes and the money collected often is used, at least in part, for maintenance and repair. Some more-formal organizations are listed below, and if they are not directly involved in funding or aiding preservation efforts, they often know who is. Websites are current at the time of publication of this book.

Archdiocese of Santa Fe Office of Historic Patrimony and Archives, www.archdiosf.org/archives

Cornerstones Community Partnerships, www.cstones.org

Historic Santa Fe Foundation, www.historicsantafe.org

New Mexico Historic Preservation Division, www.nmhistoricpreservation.org

Nuevo Mexico Profundo, www.nuevo-mexico-profundo.org

Acknowledgments

More people helped me in this endeavor than I could have imagined when I started. Lyn Ray took me to San Isidro Catholic Church in Albert (pages 28 and 29) and Manuel Garcia unlocked gates for me and showed me Santiago Catholic Church in Maes (page 76). Louise and Casimiro Romo and Rose and José Sandoval showed me to and around San Antonio Catholic Church in Aurora (page 41). Clifford Regensberg of Ledoux gave me helpful information about churches in Mora County. As he did for my previous books, Frank Graziano provided information and encouragement, and Bernadette Lucero (Archdiocese of Santa Fe) and Gretchen Brock (New Mexico Historic Preservation Division) provided helpful information. The parishes of San Francisco Xavier in Clayton, Immaculate Conception and Our Lady of Sorrows in Las Vegas, and St. Anthony in Pecos were helpful in providing information, as was Ernestina Cordova of the Taos County Historical Society. Marie Romero Cash continued to provide encouragement and information. Gabreil Romero and the Tourism Office of Taos Pueblo were gracious in giving me permission to use images taken in the pueblo in this book. Rebecca Anthony and Linda Marie Carroll of La Galeria at the Shaffer in Mountainair have encouraged my work and were among the first to carry my books. Architect Jon Dick of Santa Fe has enlightened me on many architectural details. Members of the Facebook group Abandoned, History, Landscapes & Wildlife of New Mexico have also been helpful. I thank Carl Condit and James Smith of Sunstone Press for turning my writings and photographs into beautiful books.

I also am grateful to many other individuals I have met in my travels who have generously shown me and told me about their churches, and pointed me toward others I was not aware of. Their kindness and pride in their churches have been an inspiration.

Finally, my wife Sheila David provided advice, support, encouragement, patience, and company. She came with me on many of my "churching expeditions," as we call them, and encouraged me to find good churches when she did not accompany me. She advised me on photographing individual churches and helped me choose among the photographs afterwards. I am more than grateful for those gifts from her.

CHURCHES BY COUNTY

Sacred Heart Catholic Church, Moses, Union County. Early 1900s. This stone church is on private property; I am grateful to the parish in Clayton for arranging permission for me to photograph it. From New Mexico Highway 406 take the first (gravel) road north of mile-marker 18 to the west about 600 yards. Photograph taken in 2021.

St. Joseph's Catholic Church, Folsom, Union County. Early 1900s. Another stone church, which is maintained to some degree, despite its exterior appearance. At 626 Dodge Street (off New Mexico Highway 456). Photograph taken in 2021.

St. Francis Xavier Catholic Parish Church, Clayton, Union County. 1937. This Romanesque-revival church, recently restored and usually open to visitors, is not typically New Mexican. At 115 North 1st Street. Photograph taken in 2021.

The interior of St. Francis Xavier Church. The tasteful restoration does not reflect New Mexican influence, but the church is only about ten miles from Texas and Oklahoma. Photograph taken in 2021.

Our Lady of Guadalupe Catholic Church, Des Moines, Union County. 1954. The church, built of large bricks, is at 818 Broadway Avenue (U.S. Highway 87) just west of 2nd Street. Photograph taken in 2021.

Holy Trinity Catholic Church, Hayden, Union County. Probably built in the 1910s, the church has long been abandoned. On Hayden Road about two miles south of New Mexico Highway 102. Photograph taken in 2019.

Sacred Heart Catholic Church, Bueyeros, Harding County. 1900. This neo-Gothic stone church is visible from miles away, like a battleship at sea. On New Mexico Highway 102. Photograph taken in 2019.

St. Joseph's Catholic Church, Mosquero, Harding County. 1913. The orange color of the roof is quite recent (and striking). At 45 Cedar Street. Photograph taken in 2019.

San Isidro Catholic Church, Albert, Harding County. Late 1800s. The adobe church is on the privately owned Tequesquite Ranch. It is beautifully maintained, but not currently used for services. Photograph taken in 2022.

The beautifully maintained interior of San Isidro Catholic Church in Albert. Most of the art and material are original. Notice the carved beam. Photograph taken in 2022.

Immaculate Conception Catholic Church, Gallegos Ranch, Harding County. 1914. Apparently, the church that predated this stone, neo-Gothic church was destroyed by a tornado. Just off New Mexico Highway 39 on private property. Photograph taken in 2022.

San Antonio Catholic Church, Logan, Quay County. Around 1910. This fairly traditional adobe church is at 907 Armijo Street. The large vestibule likely was added later. Photograph taken in 2019.

Sacred Heart Catholic Church, Nara Visa, Quay County. Around 1900. This attractive wooden church is only three miles from the Texas border, and has no strong regional character. On North 6th Street loop off North 5th Street (New Mexico Highway 402). Photograph taken in 2020.

Joana Darca (Joan of Arc) Catholic Church, Montoya, Quay County. Early 1900s. A plaque says the small, abandoned church is in memory of Cirilio Martinez. Exit 311 north off Interstate 40, then Frontage Road to the northeast. The church is down a short road to the right. Photograph taken in 2020.

Sagrada Familia (Holy Family) Catholic Church, Newkirk, Guadalupe County. Early 1900s. Sadly abandoned and vandalized. Newkirk, ironically, is an anglicized surname meaning new church. Exit 300 off Interstate 40 on the north side. Photograph taken in 2022.

San José Catholic Church, Colonias, Guadalupe County. 1780s with later additions. The once-grand adobe church seems too far gone to be restored. From Exit 267 off Interstate 40 take Colonias Road (New Mexico Highway 379) about 12 miles to Romero Street to the church. Photograph taken in 2021.

Santo Niño de Atocha Catholic Chapel, Dahlia, Guadalupe County. Early 1900s. Nine miles down the mostly gravel Dahlia Road from New Mexico Highway 386, then right on Capello Road 1.6 miles. The adobe chapel is visible several hundred yards to the left on private property. Photograph taken in 2019.

San José Catholic Church, Anton Chico, Guadalupe County. 1857/1929. The twin steeples of this striking adobe church can be seen from far away. Take New Mexico Highway 386 to Anton Chico Road, then right on Chili Road. Photograph taken in 2019.

Sacred Heart Catholic Church, Dilia, Guadalupe County. 1900. This lovely adobe church is on New Mexico Highway 119 just west of U.S. Highway 84. Photograph taken in 2019.

Sangre de Cristo Catholic Church, Upper Anton Chico, Guadalupe County. 1834. This charming adobe church, like those at Dilia and Anton Chico (preceding pages), is near the Pecos River. It is just east of New Mexico Highway 386. Photograph taken in 2019.

Nuestra Señora de Guadalupe Catholic Church, Tecolotito, San Miguel County. 1945. The adobe church has had some restoration. Tecolotito means little owl. South on County Road B45B from New Mexico Highway 386 to Calle Feliz. Photograph taken in 2019.

San Antonio Catholic Church, Aurora, San Miguel County. 1920s. A four-foot-tall statue of San Antonio from this now-abandoned stone church is in a nearby home. The church received a new roof in 2000, but restoration seems unlikely now. About 1.5 miles west on County Road B36 from New Mexico Highway 3, then on private property to the south. Photograph taken in 2021.

Santa Mission (formerly Our Lady of Guadalupe) Catholic Church, Sabinoso, San Miguel County. Late 1800s. The church is in an extremely isolated, tiny community, one of those places at the end of the road. About six miles up County Road C55A from New Mexico Highway 419. Photograph taken in 2019.

San Antonio Mission Catholic Church, Las Vegas, San Miguel County. 1886. A traditional, small, adobe church with neo-Gothic windows. At 86 Old National Road. Photograph taken in 2019.

Immaculate Conception Catholic Church, Las Vegas, San Miguel County. 1949. The large, neo-Gothic brick church is at 811 6th Street. Photograph taken in 2021.

The interior of Immaculate Conception Catholic Church. The 1992 renovation of the interior won a Best Restored Building of the Year award. Photograph taken in 2021.

Our Lady of Sorrows Catholic Church, Las Vegas, San Miguel County. 1885. This Romanesque stone church would not seem out of place in the midwestern United States. At 450 West National Avenue. Photograph taken in 2022.

The interior of Our Lady of Sorrows in Las Vegas. Notice the carved statues of saints (bultos) on the supports. Photograph taken in 2022.

Santo Niño Catholic Church, Los Alamos, San Miguel County. Early 1900s. This otherwise traditional adobe church is strikingly asymmetrical. From Exit 352 north ("Airport") off Interstate 25, 3.7 miles north on County Road A6 to an unlocked gate, then 0.3 miles to the church. Photograph taken in 2021.

The interior of Santo Niño Catholic Church does not show the striking asymmetry of the exterior. The latillas in the ceiling form a lovely herring-bone pattern. Photograph taken in 2021.

San Isidro Labrador Catholic Church, Gonzales Ranch, San Miguel County. 1932. Despite its whitewashed façade, the church is built of stone. On San Isidro Lane off County Road B30B near its junction with County Road B31A. Photograph taken in 2020.

San Francisco de Asís Catholic Church, near Leyba, San Miguel County. Early 1900s. This remote adobe church is surrounded by a cemetery. Take County Road B31A to B31D, then after sharp left turn through an unlocked gate, 0.9 mile to the church. Photograph taken in 2020.

Catholic Chapel of Santa Rita de Cascia, Bernal, San Miguel County. 1917. This appealing stone chapel has a separate bell structure. Exit 330 off Interstate 25 to County Road B26A, then left to the chapel. Photograph taken in 2019.

Nuestra Señora del Rosario Catholic Church, Lagunita, San Miguel County. Around 1900. The stone church is in a tiny community that never had more than a few inhabitants. Continue past the Chapel of Santa Rita (opposite) to County Road 27A; the church is about eight miles past the turnoff. Photograph taken in 2019.

San Agustín Catholic Church, Los Valles de San Agustín, San Miguel County. Mid–1800s. The church, in a tiny settlement in the lovely Gallinas River Valley, was beautifully restored recently. Exit 343 off Interstate 25 south on Frontage Road, to County Road C24 just past mile-marker 1, across the railroad tracks 8.5 miles to the church. Photograph taken in 2020.

La Concepción Catholic Church, Lourdes, San Miguel County. Around 1880. Fairly similar to San Agustín, the adobe church was restored in the 1990s but has since been abandoned. About three miles down County Road C24 past San Agustín. Photograph taken in 2020.

Nuestra Señora de los Desamparados Catholic Church, El Cerrito, San Miguel County. 1886. This classic adobe church is in a charming, much-studied village on the Pecos River. On County Road B28/B28A about ten miles south from Bernal; or B28A east from New Mexico Highway 3 near Villanueva. Photograph taken in 2019.

Our Lady of Guadalupe Catholic Church, Villanueva, San Miguel County. 1818-1826. This attractive stone church is in the church plaza just off New Mexico Highway 3. Photograph taken in 2019.

Nuestro Señor de Esquípulas Catholic Church, Sena, San Miguel County. 1900. This striking, well-maintained adobe church has a separate bell tower with its own corrugated-iron roof. On County Road B58 about 600 yards west of New Mexico Highway 3. The turnoff is between mile markers 63 and 64. Photograph taken in 2019.

Small, private chapel just east of Nuestro Señor de Esquípulas (opposite); Sena, San Miguel County. Although it looks older, it was built in the 1980s, and was demolished in 2020. *Sic transit gloria mundi*. Photograph taken in 2019.

San Antonio de Padua Catholic Church, El Pueblo (Ribera), San Miguel County. 1906. This traditional adobe church is just to the east of New Mexico Highway 3 on St. Anthony's Lane. Photograph taken in 2019.

St. Anthony of Padua Catholic Church, Pecos, San Miguel County. 1906. This stone, neo-Gothic church replaced an earlier adobe one and was inspired, even after his death, by Santa Fe Archbishop Jean Baptiste Lamy's preference for French over New Mexican style. On St. Anthony's Loop. Photograph taken in 2019.

Nuestra Señora de Guadalupe Catholic Church, El Macho, San Miguel County. 1856. Small and charming, the adobe church is just across New Mexico Highway 63 from the Pecos River, about seven miles north of Pecos. Photograph taken in 2019.

San Miguel del Vado Catholic Church, Ribera, San Miguel County. 1806. Clearly designed in part to be a fortress, this large, handsome, adobe church is on Sagebrush Way at New Mexico Highway 3. Photograph taken in 2019.

Our Lady of Guadalupe Catholic Church, South San Ysidro (Ilfeld), San Miguel County. Around 1930. This ornate adobe church has carved portico supports and a decorated façade with a painting of Our Lady of Guadalupe. At 229 County Road B43B. Exit 307 or 323 off Interstate 25, take Frontage Road to the county road. Photograph taken in 2019.

San Isidro Labrador Catholic Church, North San Ysidro, San Miguel County. Around 1900. The traditional adobe church is in a small settlement on the Pecos River. Continue on County Road B43B about three miles past Our Lady of Guadalupe. Photograph taken in 2020.

San Isidro Catholic Church, Trujillo, San Miguel County. 1940. The stone church was built by community members after a budget of $100 proved inadequate, even in 1940. On County Road C51A just off New Mexico Highway 104. Photograph taken in 2019.

Holy Family Catholic Church, Variadero (Garita), San Miguel County. 1910. This traditional, whitewashed adobe church is on New Mexico Highway 104 near the Conchas River. Photograph taken in 2019.

San Rafael Catholic Church, Trementina, San Miguel County. Around 1905. Small and traditional, the whitewashed adobe church has a cemetery with a lovely bed of irises. From New Mexico Highway 419 take County Road C56A north a few miles through a private ranch to the church. Photograph taken in 2019.

Nuestra Señora de los Angeles de Porciúncula Catholic Church, Pecos National Historical Park, San Miguel County. 1717. These ruins are on the site of an even larger church built in 1625, destroyed in the Pueblo Revolt of 1680. On Peach Drive off New Mexico Highway 63. Photograph taken in 2020.

Santo Niño de Atocha Catholic Church, La Manga, San Miguel County. 1932. The adobe church has a separate bell tower and an unusual green roof. Exit 339 off Interstate 25; in front of the gas station head west on Frontage Road 2116 to La Manga Trail to the church. Photograph taken in 2019.

Nuestra Señora de Guadalupe Catholic Church, Ojitos Fritos, San Miguel County. Late 1800s. The traditional adobe church does not appear to be used and needs repair. Exit 339 off Interstate 25; in front of the gas station head northeast on Frontage Road 2116, which becomes County Road A20/Ojitos Fritos Road. Continue about six miles to the church. Photograph taken in 2021.

San José de Gracia Catholic Church, San José, San Miguel County. Around 1880. The statues in front of the traditional, adobe church are distinctive. Exit 319 off Interstate 25 to Frontage Road 2116 to the east, then County Road B41D under the freeway to the church. Photograph taken in 2020.

San Juan Nepomucemo Catholic Church, San Juan, San Miguel County. Early 1900s. Both this church and San José are very close to the Pecos River. Exit 319 off Interstate 25 to the gas station, then County Road B41A to the church. Photograph taken in 2020.

Our Lady of Sorrows Catholic Church, Tecolote, San Miguel County. 1838. Notice the separate bell tower with the cross; there is no cross on the steeple of this whitewashed, adobe church. Exit 335 off Interstate 25, then left on County Road B47A into the village and the church. Photograph taken in 2019.

San Antonio de Padua Catholic Church, Los Montoyas, San Miguel County. Likely early 1900s. This traditional church is at 770 U.S. Highway 84, about ten miles south of Exit 339 off Interstate 25. Photograph taken in 2019.

Santiago (St. James) Catholic Church, Maes, San Miguel County. 1890s. The church is surrounded by private land whose owner prevents access to it by locked gates across the road. New Mexico Highway 104 east to County Road C53A then left on County Road C53B to locked gates. Photograph taken in 2019.

Cristo Rey Catholic Church, El Llano, San Miguel County. Probably built around 1920, painted much later. The church provides a marvelous splash of color in an uncolorful landscape. On the east side of New Mexico Highway 65 about seven miles north of Las Vegas. Photograph taken in 2020.

Nuestra Señora del Refugio Catholic Church, Los Vigiles, San Miguel County. 1820. This traditional church has neo-Gothic windows. Take 8th Street north from Las Vegas; the church is about two miles past the city limits, not far after the road bends left. Photograph taken in 2022.

San José Catholic Church, Montezuma, San Miguel County. About 1900. Our Lady of Guadalupe was painted on the side of this adobe church in the 1960s. It is now used as a morada by the Penitente Brotherhood. Take St. Joseph Drive off New Mexico Highway 65 just west of the hot springs. Photograph taken in 2020.

Sagrada Familia Catholic Church, Rowe, San Miguel County. 1894. A simple, graceful execution of the northern New Mexico adobe church vernacular. Take Exit 307 off Interstate 25 to Frontage Road 2116 to Ilfeld Frontage Road. Photograph taken in 2019.

Catholic Capilla (Chapel) de Santo Niño, Gallinas, San Miguel County. 1936. This attractive chapel with a broken cross is on New Mexico Highway 65. Photograph taken in 2020.

San Antonio Catholic Church, El Porvenir, San Miguel County. Likely 1930s. The church, with its neo-Gothic windows, is surrounded by trees. Follow New Mexico Highway 65 past Gallinas to a right turn also labeled Highway 65; it is less than a mile to the church. Photograph taken in 2020.

San Ignacio Catholic Church, San Ignacio, San Miguel County. 1862. The whitewashed adobe church is partly obscured by trees. From New Mexico Highway 94 take New Mexico Highway 266 along the Sapello River to County Road A3A to the church. Photograph taken in 2019.

San Isidro Catholic Church, Manuelitas, San Miguel County. Mid-1800s. This abandoned stone church is not in Sapello, a few miles away, although its replacement is. About 3.5 miles up New Mexico Highway 94 from its junction with New Mexico Highway 518. Photograph taken in 2021.

Nuestra Señora de Guadalupe Catholic Church, Sapello, San Miguel County. 1940s. This adobe church replaced San Isidro in Manuelitas. Just south of the junction of New Mexico Highway 94 with New Mexico Highway 518 take the gravel road to the east to the church. Photograph taken in 2021.

La Iglesia (Catholic Church) de San Antonio, Tapia, San Miguel County. Around 1900. The adobe church was built, along with the nearby cemetery, by the Tapia family. About four miles north of Interstate 40 on U.S. Highway 285 take Los Cavos Lane to the east. After 2.8 miles, take the left turn 1.3 miles to the church. Photograph taken in 2021.

San Gerónimo Catholic Church, San Gerónimo, San Miguel County. Mid–1800s. This is a classic New Mexico vernacular adobe church. Exit 343 from Interstate 25, west on Frontage Road to New Mexico Highway 283 north, then left at Mile Marker 8 onto County Road A17 to the church. Photograph taken in 2019.

Santo Niño Catholic Church, Lower Rociada, San Miguel County. 1861. The area was hit hard by forest fires in 2022, but the whitewashed adobe church was not damaged. About a mile down New Mexico Highway 276 from its junction with New Mexico Highway 105. Photograph taken in 2020.

San José Catholic Church, Upper Rociada, San Miguel County. 1862. This adobe church, a few miles from Santo Niño, also was spared by the forest fires of 2022. The church is less than two miles up New Mexico Highway 105 past its junction with New Mexico Highway 276. Photograph taken in 2021.

Sacred Heart Catholic Church, Watrous, Mora County. 1907. A fine example of a New Mexico vernacular adobe church. Exit 364 or 366 off Interstate 25 onto New Mexico Highway 161 toward Watrous to the church. Photograph taken in 2019.

San Acacio de las Golondrinas Catholic Church, Golondrinas, Mora County. 1862. The cross was broken when I took this photograph, but otherwise the adobe church appeared to be in good condition. Golondrinas means swallows in Spanish. On New Mexico Highway 161 by the Mora River. Photograph taken in 2019.

Santa Clara Catholic Church, Wagon Mound, Mora County. 1930s. The stone church is at the corner of Nolan and Ritch Streets. Photograph taken in 2021.

The recently restored interior of Santa Clara Catholic Church. Photograph taken in 2021.

Santo Niño Catholic Church, Buena Vista, Mora County. 1876. Although little is distinctive about this adobe church, it does have some charm. Near the junction of county roads 11 and 12. Photograph taken in 2019.

Nuestra Señora de Guadalupe Catholic Church, Ocate, Mora County. 1900. This large adobe church is in a very sparsely populated area. Near the junction of New Mexico highways 120 and 442. Photograph taken in 2019.

San Rafael Catholic Church, La Cueva, Mora County. 1862–1870. This adobe church, whose history and recent restoration were discussed extensively by Frank Graziano (see reading list), is used occasionally. From New Mexico Highway 518 take New Mexico Highway 442 north, then the first right. Photograph taken in 2021.

San Isidro Catholic Church, Ojo Feliz, Mora County. 1900. Neither this attractive adobe church nor its village are visible from the main highway. From New Mexico Highway 442 take County Road C003 (Ojo Feliz Road). Photograph taken in 2019.

Sagrado Corazón Catholic Church, Rainsville, Mora County. 1910. Notice the red heart on the gate to this adobe church. From New Mexico Highway 442 take County Road A028 to County Road A027 (or County Road A027 directly); the church is on the left. Photograph taken in 2019.

Santo Niño Catholic Church, Monte Aplanado, Mora County. 1830s. One of the many classic, New Mexico vernacular adobe churches in the area. Although many are similar, no two are identical. From New Mexico Highway 94 a little more than a mile south of Mora take Monte Aplanado Road to the west, then right on Pacheco Village Road. Photograph taken in 2019.

San José Catholic Church, Ledoux, Mora County. 1906. The strikingly pink adobe church is on New Mexico Highway 94 about four miles south of its junction with New Mexico Highway 518 in Mora. Photograph taken in 2019.

Nuestra Señora del Carmen, North Carmen, Mora County. 1900. This attractive adobe church can be seen from quite a distance. From New Mexico Highway 94 about four miles south of Ledoux take County Road A011 toward Puercito; the church is on County Road A014 to the left. Photograph taken in 2019.

San José Catholic Church, Cañoncito, Mora County. Early 1900s. This small church is on private property just south of New Mexico Highway 518 about four miles east of Mora. Photograph taken in 2019.

Santiago del Talca Catholic Chapel, Mora, Mora County. 1900. This attractive chapel, with its blue accents and roof, is on a hill just south of Mora. From New Mexico Highway 518 on the east side of town take County Road A032. Photograph taken in 2019.

San Antonio de Padua Catholic Church, Cleveland, Mora County. Late 1800s/1982. The deteriorating old church was demolished, and many of its parts were used to build the new church, completed in 1982. The new church is very similar, but not identical, to the old one. On New Mexico Highway 518. Photograph taken in 2019.

San Ysidro Catholic Church, Vallecitos, Mora County. Late 1800s. Ownership of this stone church was transferred from the Archdiocese of Santa Fe to a private party long ago. Take Encinal Road from Cleveland to Encinal Canyon Road, then 1.9 miles from Cleveland go left up rough, unpaved Los Villecitos Road 1.3 miles. Photograph taken in 2021.

Agua Negra Presbyterian Church, Holman, Mora County. Late 1800s or early 1900s. This abandoned, Protestant church is included here because it has been misidentified as San Isidro Catholic Church. It is locally famous for an image of Christ that appeared on a wall in 1976. South of New Mexico Highway 518 just west of mile marker 35. Photograph taken in 2020.

Sacred Heart of Mary Catholic Church, Holman, Mora County. 1941. Across the parking lot from the white church opposite. An earlier Catholic mission here was named for San Isidro, possibly accounting for the confusion with the white church. Photograph taken in 2020.

Capilla de San Antonio (Catholic Chapel), Chacon, Mora County. 1865. This unusual adobe chapel is on a hill on the right off New Mexico Highway 121, six miles north of New Mexico Highway 518 just past the Post Office. Photograph taken in 2019.

Santa Rita Catholic Church, Lucero, Mora County. 1886. A classic New Mexico adobe church, it is 1.5 miles down Lucero Road off New Mexico Highway 442 just north of mile marker 5. Photograph taken in 2020.

San Juan Bautista Catholic Church, Los Hueros, Mora County. Around 1900. A traditional, whitewashed adobe church, San Juan Bautista is about 3.2 miles down Los Hueros Road off New Mexico Highway 442 near mile marker 18. Photograph taken in 2020.

Nuestro Señor de Esquípulas Catholic Church, Los LeFebres, Mora County. Around 1900. The ornate cross and buttresses, among other features, distinguish this adobe church from several others in the region. From New Mexico Highway 120 about five miles northwest of its junction with New Mexico Highway 442, take Los LeFebres Road to the southeast about two miles. Photograph taken in 2020.

Santa Teresita del Niño Jesus Catholic Church, El Turquillo, Mora County. 1920. This attractive adobe church, restored recently, is surrounded by its cemetery. On New Mexico Highway 434. Photograph taken in 2020.

Our Lady of Guadalupe Catholic Church, Guadalupita, Mora County. 1957. This church, on New Mexico Highway 434, is included because of its striking design and setting. Photograph taken in 2020.

Our Lady of Mt. Carmel Catholic Church, Palo Blanco, Colfax County. Early 1900s. This extremely remote church is beautifully maintained. From U.S. Highway 56/412 take New Mexico Highway 193 (partly unpaved) 15.2 miles north. Photograph taken in 2021.

The interior of Our Lady of Mt. Carmel Catholic Church. The rich color of the ceiling and pews gives a very warm ambience. Photograph taken through a glass window in the door in 2021.

St. Patrick's Catholic Church, Raton, Colfax County. 1907. This stone, Romanesque-revival building is now a St. Vincent de Paul thrift shop. At 401 South 4th Street. Photograph taken in 2020.

St. Joseph's/St. Patrick's Catholic Church, Raton, Colfax County. 1958. The two parishes merged and are served by this church, while St. Joseph's became the thrift store. At 105 Buena Vista Street. Photograph taken in 2020.

Catholic Chapel of San Isidro, Tinaja, Colfax County. Early 1900s. Notice the unusual support of the bell tower on this very remote adobe chapel. Take Exit 435 off Interstate 25, follow Tinaja Road 2.5 miles, then left on County Road A9 for 5.5 miles, then right 0.3 mile. Photograph taken in 2021.

St. Joseph's Catholic Church, Springer, Colfax County. 1924. This handsome, large church, formerly painted white, is at 605 5th Street. Photograph taken in 2020.

Holy Child Catholic Chapel, near Rayardo, Colfax County. 1904 or earlier. The adobe chapel is on New Mexico Highway 21. Photograph taken in 2020.

St. Mel's Catholic Church, Eagle Nest, Colfax County. About 1940. St. Mel was the nephew of the better-known St. Patrick. This church was a mission of nearby St. Patrick's, which burned down in 1956. At 200 Willow Creek Drive. Photograph taken in 2021.

Catholic Church of the Immaculate Conception, Cimarron, Colfax County. 1890. This neo-Gothic church is beautifully maintained. At 440 West 18th Street. Photograph taken in 2021.

The interior of the Immaculate Conception Church. The church was open for cleaning on this day. Photograph taken in 2021.

San Antonio Mission Catholic Church, Black Lake, Colfax County. Late 1800s. Unusually, no cross was visible on the exterior of the adobe church. About six miles south of Angel Fire on New Mexico Highway 434, turn west on Forest Road ("NF") 6, then left (south) on San Antonio Road 0.5 mile. Photograph taken in 2021.

The interior of San Antonio Church. Notice the stove for heat at this high elevation. The interior is simple but neat. Photograph taken in 2021.

Santo Niño Catholic Church, Amalia, Taos County. 1914. This wooden church is on New Mexico Highway 196 5.5 miles east of Costilla in a lovely valley on Costilla Creek. Photograph taken in 2021.

Sagrado Corazón Catholic Church, Costilla, Taos County. 1890. This adobe church, with some neo-Gothic elements, is 0.8 mile down Garcia Road from New Mexico Highway 522. Photograph taken in 2021.

Nuestra Señora de Guadalupe Catholic Church, Cerro, Taos County. 1940. This rather odd adobe church has two towers and a bell under one roof. West 1.3 miles on New Mexico Highway 378 from New Mexico Highway 522. Photograph taken in 2021.

San Antonio de Padua Catholic Church, Questa, Taos County. Built between 1865 and 1875 and recently restored or rebuilt, the adobe church is reached by heading east on Cisneros Road off New Mexico Highway 522. Photograph taken in 2021.

San Cristóbal Catholic Church, San Cristóbal, Taos County. 1937. To reach the adobe church, head east from New Mexico Highway 522 on Forest Road 493, then to Camino del Media. Photograph taken in 2021.

Santísima Trinidad (Holy Trinity) Catholic Church, Arroyo Seco, Taos County. 1834. This handsome adobe church was restored in the 1990s. Just off New Mexico Highway 150 in Arroyo Seco. Photograph taken in 2019.

Nuestra Señora de los Dolores Catholic Church, Arroyo Hondo, Taos County. Early 1830s. The shingled façade, neo-Gothic windows, and belfry were later additions. From New Mexico Highway 522 head east one mile on County Road B143 (Hondo Seco Road). Photograph taken in 2021.

San Antonio de Padua Catholic Church, Valdez, Taos County. 1823. The shingled façade and general style of this adobe church remind me of the church at Arroyo Hondo. Take New Mexico Highway 150 2.4 miles north from New Mexico Highway 230 to the T-junction; go right 0.8 mile to the church, on San Antonio Lane. Photograph taken in 2022.

Santo Niño Catholic Church, El Prado (Taos), Taos County. 1930s. To reach the church, head south on Upper Colonias Road from New Mexico Highway 522, then east on Santo Niño Road. Photograph taken in 2021.

Santa Teresa de Jesus Chapel, El Prado (Taos), Taos County. Early 1900s. This typical New Mexican adobe chapel is on U.S. Highway 64 less than two miles north of the Taos plaza. Photograph taken in 2019.

Ruin of San Gerónimo Catholic Church, Taos Pueblo, Taos County. 1726. The church was largely destroyed in 1847 by U.S. artillery fire during the Taos Revolt against U.S. occupation of New Mexico. The ruin has been left as a memorial. At the western wall of the pueblo; this 2022 photograph used here by permission of Taos Pueblo.

San Gerónimo Catholic Church, Taos Pueblo, Taos County. 1850. This adobe church, which was remodeled in 1920, replaced the old one. It has some striking 19th century art inside. Near the main entrance to the pueblo. This 2022 photograph used here by permission of Taos Pueblo.

San Antonio de Padua Catholic Capilla, Taos, Taos County. 1875. The small adobe chapel is in the historic La Loma Plaza, closely surrounded by other buildings. Take Valdez Lane off Ranchitos Road. Photograph taken in 2022.

Immaculate Conception Catholic Church, Ranchito (Taos), Taos County. 1867. The adobe church, with neo-Gothic windows and a painting of Our Lady of Guadalupe above the door, is on Upper Ranchitos Road. Photograph taken in 2021.

Nuestra Señora de Dolores, Cañon (Taos), Taos County. 1873/1917. This adobe church has a bell tower on one side and a shorter tower on the other. Head southeast on Kit Carson Road (U.S. Highway 64) from Taos, turn right on Witt Road, then right on Chapel Road. Photograph taken in 2019.

Iglesia (Catholic Church) de San Isidro, Los Cordovas (Taos), Taos County. 1832. This adobe church, partly hidden by trees, is on New Mexico Highway 240 just north of mile marker 2. Photograph taken in 2022.

San Francisco de Asís Catholic Church, Ranchos de Taos, Taos County. 1772–1815. This spectacular adobe church, with its massive buttresses, is beautifully maintained inside and out. In the plaza about four miles south of Taos, just off New Mexico Highway 68. Photograph taken in 2021.

The stunning interior of San Francisco de Asís Catholic Church. The church's structure, including carved corbels; and the art, including the altar screens; create an impression that is hard to describe and to capture in a photograph. Photograph taken in 2022.

San Juan de los Lagos Catholic Church, Talpa, Taos County. 1828. This small, pueblo-style adobe church is on New Mexico Highway 518 about 1.8 miles from its junction with New Mexico Highway 68. Photograph taken in 2021.

La Capilla de Nuestra Señora de del Carmen, Llano Quemado, Taos County. 1864. The adobe chapel is less than half a mile southeast down New Mexico Highway 382 (Old Route 382) from its junction with New Mexico Highway 68. Photograph taken in 2021.

Our Lady of Sorrows Catholic Church, Taos, Taos County. 1800s. Also known as the Placitas Chapel, and currently the Love Apple Restaurant's dining room, additional construction and vegetation have somewhat obscured its origin as a church. At 803 Paseo Pueblo del Norte (U.S. Highway 64), less than two miles north of the plaza. Photograph taken in 2023.

Selected Further Readings

Archdiocese of Santa Fe. 1998. *Four Hundred Years of Faith: Seeds of Struggle, Harvest of Faith*. An information-filled history of the Catholic Church in New Mexico with information about every parish in the archdiocese and photographs of each parish church.

Brewer, Robert, and Steve McDowell. 1990. *The Persistence of Memory: New Mexico's Churches*, Museum of New Mexico Press. A historical approach with idiosyncratically chosen photographic illustrations. The emphasis is on northern New Mexico.

Cash, Marie Romero. 1993. *Built of Earth and Song: Churches of Northern New Mexico. A Guide*. Red Crane Books. With monochrome photographs and maps. About 80 churches are pictured and more are mentioned. Many of them are in this book. Cash is a noted *santera* (church artist). Her expertise and insight make her book valuable for anyone interested in New Mexico's historic Catholic churches.

Cunningham, Elizabeth. 2011. *Historic Churches of Taos and Northern New Mexico: A Self-Guided Driving Tour of 24 Historic Iglesias*. Taos County Lodgers Association and the Town of Taos. A helpful booklet, with illustrations; a map; directions; and brief histories, including construction dates, for each of 24 churches. Available at the Taos Visitor Center, also on line at https://taos.org/explore/landmarks/churches/

Dakin, William. 2013. *Rural Churches of Northern New Mexico: A Personal Selection*. Beech River Books. A charming book of Dakin's paintings of churches, with descriptions and rough directions to them. The book has some errors in church identifications and construction materials, but it helped me considerably.

DeLorme Publishing. 2019. *New Mexico Atlas and Gazetteer*, 8th edition.

Drain, Thomas, and David Wakely. 1994. *A Sense of Mission: Historic Churches of the Southwest*. Chronicle Books. Covers several mission churches in Texas, New Mexico, and California, and one small adobe church in Colorado. Drain wrote the text and Wakely took the color photographs.

Gibson, Daniel. 2011. *Pueblos of the Rio Grande: A Visitor's Guide*. Rio Nuevo Publishers. Covers all 19 of New Mexico's active pueblos, most of which have historic churches, and includes useful information for visitors to the pueblos.

Graziano, Frank. 2019. *Historic Churches of New Mexico Today*. Oxford University Press. An in-depth look at the history of Catholicism and Catholic churches in New Mexico with an emphasis on current conditions. This excellent book has few illustrations of churches but provides detailed directions to quite a few of them.

Iowa, Jeremy. 1985. *Ageless Adobe: History and Preservation in Southwestern Architecture*. Sunstone Press. A history of southwestern architectural styles, with a strong focus on New Mexico and covering far more than only adobe. No church in this book is discussed in any detail, but the book covers locations and the architectural styles of many of them. The part on historic preservation likely will be useful to those undertaking such projects, although more-recent works should be consulted as well.

Jaramillo, Victor Dan. 2019. *Los Chimayosos: A Community History*. Outskirts Press. Jaramillo, a lifelong resident of Chimayó, writes with personal and scholarly knowledge about a northern New Mexico community, including many of its churches. With monochrome photographs.

Julyan, Robert. 1998. *The Place Names of New Mexico*, 2nd Edition. University of New Mexico Press. An indispensable guide, written with insight, humor, and great erudition.

Kessell, John. 2012. *The Missions of New Mexico Since 1776*. Sunstone Press. First published in 1980 by the University of New Mexico Press. Kessell writes engagingly and authoritatively about New Mexico's surviving mission churches, including several in this book. Illustrated with drawings, photographs, and maps.

Lehmberg, Stanford. 2005. *Churches for the Southwest: The Ecclesiastical Architecture of John Gaw Meem*. Norton. An illustrated and analytical catalogue of the famous New Mexico architect's work on churches.

Lux, Annie, and Daniel Nadelbach. 2007. *Historic New Mexico Churches*. Gibbs Smith Press. Informative histories of a selection of churches graced with Nadelbach's glorious color photographs.

Museum of New Mexico Press. 1994. *The Churches of New Mexico: The Postcard Archive Series*. Historic monochrome photographs in postcard form of some New Mexico Catholic churches from the museum's extensive collection. The photographs are dated from 1882 to 1975, with a few undated ones.

Nava, Margaret. 2004. *Along the High Road: A Guide to the Scenic Route Between Española and Taos*. Sunstone Press. A useful guide to the history, art, and culture of the region, including information about lodging and restaurants that is still useful nearly 20 years later. It describes several historic Catholic churches. With monochrome photographs.

New Mexico Historical Records Survey. 1940. Reprinted by Prenava Books, India, no date. Directory of Churches and Religious Organizations in New Mexico. This useful compilation covers all denominations that were in New Mexico at the time.

Pallen, C.B., and J.J. Wynne, editors. 1929. *The New Catholic Dictionary*. The Universal Knowledge Foundation. More an encyclopedia than a dictionary, this is an informative and authoritative compilation of all matters Catholic in the first third of the twentieth century, including information about New Mexico.

Policansky, David. 2022. *Historic Catholic Churches Along the Rio Grande in New Mexico*. Sunstone Press. Similar in format to this book, with color photographs and detailed directions to the churches. Covers the historic churches along and near the great river from the southern border of New Mexico to Taos County.

_____. 2022. *Historic Catholic Churches of Central and Southern New Mexico*. Sunstone Press. Similar in format to this book, with color photographs and detailed directions to the churches. Covers the historic Catholic churches in New Mexico south of Interstate 40 except for those along and near the Rio Grande, which are in the first book. These two books cover churches in areas adjacent to those in this book.

Glossary of Spanish Terms and Names

Adobe: Building material made from earth and organic material.

Acacio: Acacius, Greek priest of the 3rd century, also a soldier of that name who was martyred. Also 5th century Turkish priest who commanded swallows (see Golondrinas) not to impede his sermon. The name means thorny tree in Greek, and its feminine form (Acacia) also is the name of a widespread genus of trees, usually thorny, found in the southwestern U.S. and elsewhere.

Agustín: Augustine. Saint Augustine of Hippo, North Africa, 354–430 AD.

Ana: Ann, Anne. Saint Anne was Mary's mother, Jesus's grandmother.

Antonio: Anthony. Saint Anthony of Padua, born in Lisbon 1195, died 1231 in Padua.

Arroyo: A usually dry river bed or its gully, subject to occasional flooding.

Asís: Assisi. Town in Italy, home of Saint Francis.

Bautista: Baptist. St. John the Baptist.

Bulto: A three-dimensional carved figure of a saint, usually painted.

Camposanto: Cemetery.

Candelaria: Candelmas, the Feast of the Purification of the Blessed Virgin Mary.

Capía: Alternate spelling of capilla.

Capilla: Chapel.

Carmen: Carmel. Mount Carmel in the Holy Land, now Israel.

Clara: Clare. Saint Clare of Assisi, 1194–1253.

Concepción Immaculada or Purísima: Immaculate Conception, the Catholic doctrine that Mary was conceived free of original sin.

Corazón: Heart.

Corbel: A structure, usually of wood, supporting the end of a beam.

Cristo: Christ.

Cristóbal: Christopher, St. Christopher, 3rd century AD, martyr in the Holy Land.

Cruz (plural, cruces): Cross.

Desamparados: Abandoned ones.

Dios: God.

Dolores: Sorrows.

Esquípulas: A town in Guatemala, site of the Black Christ of Esquípulas (Nuestro Señor de Esquípulas), a darkened wooden image of Christ in the cathedral there.

Felipe: Philip. Filippo Neri: Italian priest, 1515–1595.

Francisco: Francis. Saint Francis of Assisi, died 1226; Saint Francis Xavier, Spanish Missionary, 1506–1552.

Gerónimo: Jerome. Saint Jerome, around 345–420 AD; theologian in the Roman province of Dalmatia.

Golondrinas: Swallows (birds).

Gracia: Grace. San José de Gracia, a name for Saint Joseph. See also José.

Grande: Great, large.

Gregorio: Gregory. Saint Gregory the Great, Bishop of Rome, 540–604 AD.

Iglesia: Church.

Ignacio: Ignatius. Saint Ignatius, Spanish priest, 1491–1556.

Inez: Agnes. Saint Agnes of Rome, virgin martyr, 291–304 AD.

Isidro: Isidore. Usually Saint Isidore the Farmer (Labrador), Spanish farmworker, 1082–1172.

Joana: Joan. Joan of Arc, French saint, 1412–1431. Burned at the stake, canonized in 1920.

José: Joseph. Saint Joseph, Mary's husband, legal father of Jesus.

Juan: John. Saint John the Apostle or Saint John the Baptist or Saint John of Nepomuk.

Lagos: Lakes. Our Lady of Saint John of the Lakes is a name for the Virgin Mary in the Americas.

Latilla: Small, de-barked branches used on church ceilings between beams.

Lorenzo: Lawrence. Saint Lawrence of Rome, deacon and martyr, 225–258 AD.

Luis: Aloysius. Aloysius de Gonzaga, Italian aristocrat and Jesuit, 1568–1591.

Luis Rey: Louis the King. Louis IX, king of France and saint, 1214–1270; canonized 1294.

Luz: Light. Nuestra Señora de la Luz, Our Lady of the Light, a name for the Virgin Mary.

Maria: Mary. Mother of Jesus.

Morada: Meeting house for members of the Penitente Brotherhood.

Miguel: Michael. Archangel Michael.

Nacimiento: Birth.

Nepomuceno: of Nepomuk, a town in the present-day Czech Republic. St. John of Nepomuk, 1345–1393, was drowned in the Vltava River by order of King Wenceslaus IV of Bohemia for refusing to divulge the contents of the queen's confession.

Niño: Child. Santo Niño de Atocha, Hispanic Catholic image of the Christ Child.

Nuestra Señora (de): Our Lady (of). The Virgin Mary: Usually followed by los Dolores (Sorrows), or other aspects of her life or community circumstances; or by a place name, such as Guadalupe in Mexico, where apparitions of the Virgin Mary occurred.

Parroquia: Parish church.

Patricio: Patrick. Saint Patrick of Ireland, 5th century missionary, never actually canonized.

Pedro: Peter. Saint Peter, approximately 1–66 AD, apostle and first Pope.

Porciúncula: Porziuncola, a place near Assisi with a small chapel that Saint Francis rebuilt in the 13th century on his interpretation of God's order; of great importance to Franciscans. The full name of the chapel was Our Lady Queen of the Angels, hence the name of the church in Pecos National Historical Park and of the City of Los Angeles in California.

Promesa: Promise or vow. An offer to perform some action or sacrifice in return or gratitude for the grant of a prayer request.

Rafael: Raphael. Archangel Raphael, first mentioned 3rd century BCE.

Refugio: Refuge. Our Lady of Refuge is a name for the Virgin Mary.

Rey: King.

Rio: River.

Rita: Rita. Saint Rita of Cascia, 1381–1457.

Rosa: Rose. Saint Rose of Lima, Peruvian saint, 1586–1617.

Rosario: Rosary. Nuestra Señora del Rosario or Our Lady of the Rosary is a term for the Virgin Mary.

Sagrada: Sacred, holy.

Sagrada Familia: Holy Family.

San, Santa, Santo: Saint (in a name, e.g., San Ignacio, Santa Ana).

Sangre: Blood.

Santa, Santo: Holy, also a saint or an image of a saint.

Santera, Santero: A maker of carved or painted images of saints, or, more broadly, church art.

Santiago: Saint James, through a contraction of Santo Iago to Sant'Iago. Saint James the Apostle.

Santísima: Most holy.

Señor: Lord.

Señora: Lady.

Teresa: Teresa. Saint Teresa of Avila, Spanish noblewoman, 1515–1582. But see Teresita.

Teresita: Thérèse, the French saint Thérèse of Lisieux, 1873–1897. In Spanish, Santa Teresita (or Teresa) del Niño Jesus.

Vicente de Paula: Vincent de Paul. Saint Vincent de Paul, French saint, 1581–1660.

Viga: A beam in the ceiling of an adobe building, often supported by corbels. Exposed ends of vigas projecting beyond the exterior walls are typical of Pueblo and Spanish colonial architecture, and are in some famous adobe churches in New Mexico.

Virgen: Virgin.

Ysidro: Isidore. See Isidro

Index to Churches by Location

Printed in the USA
CPSIA information can be obtained
at www.ICGtesting.com
LVHW062151050124
768254LV00019B/222